Jumping the Median

Jumping the Median

D. E. GREEN

Encircle Publications, LLC
Farmington, Maine USA

Jumping the Median Copyright ©2019 *D. E. Green*

Paperback ISBN-13: 978-1-64599-003-1
e-Book ISBN-13: 978-1-64599-004-8
Kindle ISBN-13: 978-1-64599-005-5

All rights reserved. No part of this book may be reproduced in any form by any mechanical or electronic means including storage and retrieval systems without express written permission in writing from the publisher. Brief passages may be quoted in review. Rights to individual poems and essays remain with authors.

Editor: Cynthia Brackett-Vincent
Book and book cover design: Eddie Vincent/ENC Graphics Services
Cover Images: Shutterstock.com

Printing: Walch Publishing, Portland, Maine

Mail Orders, Author Inquiries:
Encircle Publications
PO Box 187
Farmington, ME USA 04938
207-778-0467

Online orders:
encirclepub.com

CONTENTS

Acknowledgments

Dedication

Thanks

À la mode de Kahlo: The Lovers 1

A Big White Dog Stands Watch at the Back Door 2

Pink Cadillac 3

Perfect Couple 4

Course Requirement 5

No Time for Poetry 6

Road Closed 8

paradise now 9

Natural Selection 10

Grain Elevator 11

Sestina: Moonlight Fool 12

Loons 14

Small-town Summer Stalker 15

Prufrock Redux 16

Is there an I 19

School Choice 20

Chicago Heat 21

Because It Hath No Bottom 22

Don Quijote Broke My Pate 24

A Candle's Flame Quickens the Darkest Night 25

Plaza Rosada: 15 August 1990 26

End of the Line 28

Pantoum: The Western Sky 29

Rain 30

Lifeguard 31

Back Porch: Northfield, MN 35

Craft 36

Walk, Don't Run 37

Mnemosyne 38

Villanelle: Mortality's an Everyday Affair 39

Return to Me 40

Familial Rites: The Wedding 41

In Search of Poetry 43

A Visit to Theresienstadt 44

Autobiography: After Frank O'Hara 46

plenty. 47

New York School Cool 48

Geezers at the Old Saloon. 49

O Mortal Raisin! 50

The Lost Book of Hours 51

The Would-be Naturalist Goes Birding 52

Northern Winter 53

Charlie Chaplin Jumps the Median 54

Parting Glances 56

Gratitude 58

A Topography of Love 61

About the Author 62

ACKNOWLEDGMENTS

"À la mode de Kahlo: The Lovers" was published in the anthology *Rec*og*nize: The Voices of Bisexual Men—An Anthology*, ed. Robyn Ochs and Herukati (Boston: Bisexual Resources Center, 2014). The anthology was nominated for Lambda Literary Award.

"A Topography of Love" appeared online in *Writers' Night: All in the Family* 1.2 (November 2004): 31.

"Because It Hath No Bottom" appeared as Poem of the Week in the What Light Series, MNartists.org, 14 May 2007 <http://mnartists.org/article.do?rid=146658>.

"Craft," "Natural Selection," and "Perfect Couple" appeared in *Rag Mag* 17 (2001): 71-72.

"Familial Rites: The Wedding," appeared in *Sidewalks* 6 (Spring/Summer 1994): 39.

"Gratitude" appeared in *Martin Lake Journal* and won MLJ's 2017 Bookend Prize.

"Mnemosyne" and "Plaza Rosada: 15 August 1990" were published in the now defunct online journal *Three Candles*, edited by Steve Mueske in July 2001.

"Pantoum: The Western Sky," "Loons ," "Northern Winter," "Grain Elevator," and "Chicago Heat," were published in the *Great Lakes Book Project*, ed. Walter Blake Knoblock (Traverse City, MI: Felix Exi, 2013).

"Parting Glances" and "No Time for Poetry" appeared in *Rag Mag* 13.2 (Winter/Spring 1996): 5-9.

"The Would-be Naturalist Goes Birding" won the 2nd Place Prize in the Poet-Artist Collaboration XII sponsored by The Crossings, Zumbrota, MN, 19 April 2013. It was printed in the exhibit catalog with "Saturday" by artist Bobby Marines.

Between 2001 and 2015, the following poems appeared in the annual issue of Augsburg College's campus literary magazine, *Murphy Square*: "Is there an I," "Back Porch: Northfield, MN," "Autobiography: After Frank O'Hara," "paradise now," "Walk, Don't Run," "À la mode de Kahlo: The Lovers," "Rain," "Don Quijote Broke My Pate," "I pick my way" (now "School Choice"), and "plenty."

DEDICATION

For Becky, Zach, all my siblings, Mom, and Dad, who's still with me.

THANKS

Poets don't work in a vacuum. So I have many people to thank for their help: foremost among them are Cheri Johnson, Chris Kallman, Leslie Schultz, and Sarah Myers, whose comments on the first draft of the manuscript were indispensable.

I have to thank all the members of my writing groups in the Twin Cities and Northfield who read many of the poems here, especially Heather Beatty, LeRoy Sorenson, Mike McCarron, Molly Ronin Anthony, Beth Morse Lareau, Bruce Morlan, Jan Hill, Bob Tisdale, the late Dagmar Tisdale, Jane McDonnell, and Scott Carpenter, among others. Their support and critique were indispensable.

Thanks, too, to John Garrison, Heather Dubrow, and the late Eric Binnie—fellow Shakespeareans who have encouraged this creative work. All my Augsburg English Department colleagues, especially Cass Dalglish, Cary Waterman and the late John Mitchell, Augsburg's Center for Teaching and Learning, and many Augsburg students provided encouragement and support.

Thanks to poets Mike Finley, Danny Klecko, St. Paul Poet Laureate Carol Connolly, Northfield Poet Laureate Rob Hardy, and Content Books in Northfield for my earliest opportunities to read publicly.

Thanks to Encircle Publications and my editor Cynthia Brackett-Vincent for their attention and care in bringing this work to fruition.

I am deeply grateful to my son and fellow artist Zachary Boling-Green, who took an active interest in this work.

And my deepest gratitude, of course, to my more-than-writing partner Becky Boling—without whom, nothing.

À la mode de Kahlo: The Lovers

Is that a dead hummingbird on your necklace of thorns
    or are you just Frida Kahlo?
Am I supposed to put my Diego on ice, to see the real you
    behind the peasant mask and striking poses?

Sometimes love feels like incest, we get so close we merge,
    like the Cyclops eye I see when love-making brings us face to face.
What is a gay man doing in a lesbian's bed? we've wondered
    and yet found no hearth nor home in other arms.

Oh, we do imagine others' lips and sheets, phantom romance,
    the kind the airport novels offer, all heaving bosoms and protruding packets.
But still we fly home, fall into the familiar indentations, and move our fingers
    along the old well-worn grooves and levers, maneuvering

like rusty ancients on old red tractors. That's love—
    though you wouldn't think so to see us ride. If love's perennial
survives, its seeds fall in the end on untilled soil, weeds springing
    despite the unpromising and unseasonable weather.

You shouldn't have loved me, love, because I don't like
    hummingbirds, alive or dead. There's no Diego worth this show,
though your Kahlo imitation has its pleasures. Before the end,
    we will sit side by side for our portrait: the thorns drawing blood

siphoned by arteries from your heart to mine and back, cross-sections of my brain
    revealing monkeys of pleasure, a lemur wrapped around your neck
and staring back at me. That's love, my love, entwinéd *us* upon the operating table,
    Siamese twins joined at the groin, the despair of the hovering surgeon.

A Big White Dog Stands Watch at the Back Door

At night a big white dog stands watch
at the back door. Not the back door
of the house we live in now. The one
I used to live in, before I met you.

The dog stands there. Just a dog, however
big, however white. He's waiting for me
to stop worrying the threshold, to stop
watching—to move into his waiting world.

Do dogs mean anything? Should I
be looking into the kind of dog
I'm seeing in my dreams? Does it matter
whether he's a Great Pyrenees

or a Kuvasz, Maremma, or nightmare
Bichon Frise? An Argentine Dogo or
a Komondor, you know, the kind that looks
like the mop-head the old school janitors

pushed when we were kids? And why the back
door, the one that led out into the yard?
It was just a plain screen door that opened
onto crabgrass and sun-lit dandelions.

That big white dog stands watch
at the back door. Not the back door
of the house we live in now. The one
I used to live in. Before I met you.

Pink Cadillac

Through the downpour she was scurrying
toward the pink Cadillac—the best
romances always have lots of rain,
for atmosphere, a writer once told me.
So I knew, before the turning of a page,
that the book would satisfy me,
that the water running up and back
in windshield streams would lead to love,
that the pink-finned antique car
spelled sex, the kind you don't get
everyday. That's the kind of world
I want to live in, not the one where
I have to worry about putting potatoes
on the table and tucking the kids in
every night. What about desire? What
about romance? What about songbirds?
Why aren't we living in that book?
Why isn't every living page crammed
with rain and lust and a pink Cadillac?

Perfect Couple

He came from old stock, never assimilated:
ancients had pitched colorful tents—in desert.
Dispersed, they had done far more than survive
but had never fit in.

                        She came from freckled warriors
painted blue—red-haired witches brewing against
enemies and illness. Subjected, they
outlived defeat, accepted indignity
as the wages of life.

Before they'd met, they'd done it all—
at least everything *they* could think of.
He—thin and frail, nearsighted, goofy
but smart, sweet on the outside, cool within.
She—round and fair, splay-footed, shy
but smart, cool on the outside, sweet within.
Both good at their jobs, bad at being themselves.
Both good at picking bad bedfellows,
at accommodating requests.

                                They had
done a bit of this—masturbation, fornication—
and that—cunnilingus, sodomy,
fellatio, bestiality. They had
done unto others as they would have done
unto them. And vice-versa—and then some.

The only novelties? Chastity and faith:
blessings, vows, rings and veils, hearts, knees, hands, lips—
the feast after the hunt, the feast hunted after.

Course Requirement

Once I gave my underwear to a professor
of Greek. I had to—she required them,
so that she could dye them black: we were
putting on the *Ajax* by Sophocles
and I was playing Teucer (the eponymous
hero's younger brother who apparently
ran around in a little Robin Hood get-up)
and I was shy and afraid of the professor,
who was attractive and very smart and funny
and, yes, sexy and I was an idiot (still am)
and so naturally I just turned in my
underwear. I did very well in that class—
people came from all over New England
to hear us speak in the old style, in the tragic
poet's ancient Greek, and to see me
in my blackened Fruit-of-the-Looms.

No Time for Poetry

For Rick

It's not just lacking time
between the morning Nutri-Grain
and banana that will not go down
without a story concocted on the spot
to ease a three-year-old digestive tract:
there might be poetry in that.

It's not just finding time
(and taking it, or else)
to touch uninterrupted
the woman who's the reason
I stay here: sure,
there is poetry in that.

It's not the fifth committee
going nowhere, the students
lining up outside my office
to argue for a better grade,
less work, extensions, and
extenuations: humanity
there is, if not poetry, in that.

It's not even forty's looming
that silences my pen
nor the monumental ennui
always settling in,
nor this singsong rhythm
that undermines my "why"
nor inadvertent rhyming,
"why bother?" and "why try?"
Though bad, there's poetry in these.

The blame lies nearer: we have
halved ourselves, forgot the lyric
grace, the music that streams through
words and things, that sweeps us thus together—
one current flowing from Parnassus to the sea.

Road Closed

I move through dappled shadows toward "Road Closed,"
the pedals spinning faster than my speed
as if I were not moving toward the sign
its white and black illumined by the sun.

I've set my sights toward home but do not think
to reach the goal elusive from the start
since even bodies make discomfortable
dwellings—no shelter from the terrors of the earth.

Unthinkingly we pump the pedals whirring
gradually toward barriers ahead
gliding past landscapes peripheral and still
our wheels circling toward sunlight at road's end.

But sighs and signs of promised ends may lie—
The bright obscures what shadows clarify.

paradise now

there is no other Eden
never was
just the blossoms
blasted wasted
turning toward the light
and away toward death
and darkness and decay

he turns to her
takes the fruit she proffers
it is the only sustenance
an old man sleeps on the street
an old woman dozes in the park

this is Eden
here now the sagging skin
the lost thought the past
on the tip of the tongue
without savor
without consciousness

we live on death
batten on it
the bodies are buried here

we return to the scene of the crime
each day
live there

our bodies are dying now
just so much blood and dust

this is Eden
there is no other

Natural Selection

Beneath the maple still angling sixty
degrees to elude the lost elm's crown,
George (unreconstructed hippie) sculpts
rhododendrons at our backyard's far end. He
whispers to them, admires the forms he gives
them, smiles at his handiwork and Nature's,
decides that, yes, that cypress mulch will do
the trick. George redeems the frail, ensures each lives
despite our long neglect. He kneels to weed,
spreads cypress shreds our pup will gnaw. Pony-
tail falling forward over his right shoulder—
his absorption ratifies our need.
How, George, did one blasted thing survive
before you taught our garden how to thrive?

Grain Elevator

The traffic on Hiawatha
(Backdoor to the city)
Always stalls by the ADM
Elevator, trucks backed in
To load and cart the grain away.

Today I'm waiting at the light
And notice under the mammoth
Cylinders Sheeler immortalized
A small spill, a hillock of corn—
Never to be planted, boiled, or popped.

But it is already nourishing
The sparrows, a small flock
Whirling over our windshields
To land on the curbless drive
By the elevator's loading dock.

They scratch and pick,
Peck and nibble at the pile.
Each sparrow does its part.
The little mound collapses,
its elements lifted skyward.

We watch because we cannot
Move, because this little fracas
Mirrors our own small worlds,
Our immediate destinations,
Our tussle over others' leavings.

When the light changes
We look away, ease forward.
We are on our way,
Mindless of sparrows
Wheeling overhead.

Sestina: Moonlight Fool

Tonight the bright circle of the moon
mocks him sleepless. "Fool!"
Why, after half a century, does he still long
for, still whisper
his ineffable desire? A passing cloud
casts its shadow. The crickets hush,

the wee-hour birds hush.
Still there's moon-
light, wisping cloud,
a muttering fool,
an aspirated whisper:
The night is long.

The night is long and long-
ing. His lips move, shape hushed
syllables, do not rise above a whisper.
He addresses the moon,
praises her full-
ness, dappled by cloud.

But night clouds
cannot halt the dawn. Not long
till he must lay aside the fool,
forget the hush
of the mottled moon,
and cease to whisper.

The daylight creature does not whisper
hopes or prayers to clouds
or brilliant moons
of the somedays for which he longs.
Only night's hush
welcomes such a fool.

Fool,
whisper
(in this dark's deep hush
and the shadow of this cloud)
how you, sleepless, long
for the fullness of the moon.

O Moon, I am your poor fool,
longing, longing, swept by wisps and whispers
of night cloud, smitten still by your light's hush.

Loons

The loons are at it again
in the middle of the night:
hooting and quarreling,

moaning their joy and pain,
cawing commands,
shrieking like Shakespearean shrews.

I wake, worry the sheets,
toss off the twisted covers,
turn, slip under again—

sleep on edge, anticipate
the night's shrill keening.

Small-town Summer Stalker

I want to prowl like a cat
a black cat at midnight
the kind that wakes up
the neighbors doing the nasty
with the kitty next-door

I want to slink along
backstreets to see what
the hell that guy over on
6th and Union
is watching at 2 AM

I want to poison
the yappadoodle
down the block that barks
each night until the guy at 6th
and Union douses the light

I want to sneak
into Mr. Movies and hide
the DVD for tomorrow
behind some double-B flick—
my own special reserve

I want to do real bad
stuff—the stuff my mom
taught me not to do—
and I would too—I would!—
if only I could remember how.

Prufrock Redux

When dawn comes, we rise and go,
arise and go: Motion has its own reason,
its own season.

When the noon sun glares,
we survey the world from our perch
by the window: the church spire,
the city park, the stolen rental car.
You put down your pen.
I take the car for a spin.

When night falls, we return,
play solitaire at table, move
chess men perfunctorily
across the board.
We are together and alone,
present and absent,
necessary and dispensable.

        In the streets children play and run
        under the muzzle of a gun.

There will be time. There will be time
for spreadsheets, budget-balancing,
the do's and don't's of scheduling,
dating, mating, copulating.

There will be time
to walk hither and yon, to stop and go,
sleep and wake, know everything and nothing,
before we turn and turn and turn again,
somnambulists moving through dreamscapes
of others' making and our own.

        In the streets children play and run
        under the muzzle of a gun.

Tell me a story but not
the one you always tell me.
Tell me a story of pain and family and night.
Tell me of parents and horror and love,
of Oedipal delights and Clytemnestrian flights.
Tell me the story of our dying.

Lady Bracknell called yesterday
about the handbag, left her card
and an invitation to the séance.
So?
Well…
And you'd like me to do what exactly?
What is the meaning of this handbag?
Of the artifacts that ground us in the world?
My grandmother's ring—to be given
to the girl I married? Sara's ring, so tiny,
but (lost to us now) too big to comprehend?
Your ring, which once meant everything?

        In the streets children play and run
        under the muzzle of a gun.

Have they all come here to dine?
Charles, set the meal on the dining room table:
we'll picnic indoors.
We shall eat, ponder our destinies, and die:

        I decline
        I decline
        I've reached the last of my lives nine.

On the beach I heard the mermaids singing:
he has kindly killed them, killed them kindly.

Now we turn toward the house,
eat a supper of meat and starch—
four-minute beef packs, a few sprouts,
processed mashed potatoes.

The first lover throws off her shawl,
the second tosses aside his pillow.
Their object gazes out the window,
the very figure of desire.

We don't know how to end it.
We won't know how to end it.
We live in the house of the dead.

Is there an I

that speaks these lines
stands behind them
guarantees their value
weights them with worth?

Or do lines simply limn
this page because some digits
and keys have struck a chord
hum mutter mingle murmur

moan groan ache panic preen
perch wheeze giggle laugh
allude elude delude mock
murder frighten confuse

discombobulate fret
furnish elate enchant
torture nurture fracture?
What I, what you lies

behind these lines, lays
these lines, encodes decodes
the black marks on a blank
sheet that pass for meaning?

School Choice

I pick my way
over the bodies of colleagues who won't
answer their e-mail promptly, who refuse
to recognize that the end has come
and gone and that this is as god-awful
good as it gets

over now-limp administrators who had
quite another plan for my self-improvement,
higher productivity, all worked out
over lunch at a retreat in a luxe hotel in DC—
if I were in a car, I'd back up over them,
even the ones I like, because I'm tired

so tired of students who write
about weeding out the dead wood
as if post-tenure review were an academic
form of forestry or animal husbandry
as if they could come late to every class
never meet a deadline, expect that I
am waiting by the phone at 10 pm
just to field questions about how important
the Milton paper is in their grade
as a whole—and I'm thinking the only hole
is the one I want to blast between their ears

but I don't work at the post office
I don't even belong to the NRA
no, I'm just a humble intellectual
with too many ironies in the fire.

Chicago Heat

When it's 90-something in Chicago,
the breeze off the Lake gives scant relief.
Joggers and strollers rain perspiration.
In the fountains at Millenium Park,
the children splash and scream.

But on Michigan they're shooting the seventh
sequel to a bad disaster flick: At Wacker
the drawbridge is frozen open. Cars are in flames.
A helicopter shoots it all from above.

Citizens are dropping of sunstroke.
But that's no disaster:
We got to see 'em blow up Mickey Rourke.

Because It Hath No Bottom

The prophet called
but didn't leave a number.
Oh, in the beginning was the word,
but the word has splayed flesh:
*Blessed art thou among women
and blessed is the fruit of thy whom*
wot maykes it so difficoo(l)t
to get a dite on Satteday night—
even in Siloa's valley or on Parnassus' epic crags.

Put out the light and then put out the light
or the light will be the death of us,
the first curse, the "let there be"
that wouldn't let it be,
the kick of consciousness, the sting
of conscience, light from light,
true god from true god begotten,
but made, for nothing will come
of nothing, just virgins and angels
that keep holy the sabbath, that do not
take the name of the lord hither or yon,
beyond range of the signal, the sign,
we would have some sign—for we shall not be
eased till we be nothing short of
nothing.

    Why have you forsaken
us? Left us with few talents, prodigal
children all, fatted calves with no sacrifice
to attend to, except to suffer the little children
through the eye of a rich man's needle?
You laugh, but it's that hard—Shhhh! I tell only
the hawk or the handsaw, in whom silence is
an excellent thing.

      But music is a rare
brooch in this all-hating world.
A siren's song to dash us upon the rocks,
to ground us on the shallows of desire.
Panting for divinity. And yes, yes, yes, yes,
I will.

      But why? Etherized like satan, patient
at table, awaiting endlessly the end, tomorrow
and tomorrow and Tuesday next, the big sale day,
the big discount, priceless, the priceless pearl—
peerless, without number.

Don Quijote Broke My Pate

He fell unexpectedly from the shelf,
grazing my temple with his bronze spear,
impaling horse and rider in the bottom
shelf of the bookcase. The blood began to flow,
ideals to scatter to the wind like leaves
torn from unread books. How can we go on
if we don't know where we've come from, what we
have been, might be? Pundits cannot clarify
the vast La Mancha it is our fate to ride.

Later, when I'd stanched the wound, reduced
the swelling with a bit of ice, removed
the old knight to safer ground, I wondered,
Would he still permit a hungry sidekick
to follow, mule-shaken, belly grumbling quest-long
through these worlds, this universe, between us?

A Candle's Flame Quickens the Darkest Night

Seed of light. Imp of possibility.
Shadows prance, like plumed equestrians

around the circus ring, astride their graceful
mounts, arms waving. Joy moves, exuberant—

pulsing light and shade and light and shade
dazzle the eye: their dance, the rhythm of the mind.

Plaza Rosada: 15 August 1990

In Buenos Aires suns do not so much set as fade. Here
at the top of the hill in the Plaza de San Martín, sitting out
the south's mild winter evening on a stone bench, getting through
old *New Republics*, reading about the life of Simone
de Beauvoir, I find the warm pale gray transmuted—suffused
light illumining entanglements of Beauvoir and Sartre—
to palpable Argentine *rosado*.

       But here what they
call pink is not, like the peach of the Casa Rosada,
where Menem—the Peronist, euphemed Justicialist—confounds
distinctions between left and right. Which brings me back to Sartre
and Beauvoir: if that was not marriage, then what is?
Yet they refused the term.

       Hidden, too,
in my bag (because I cannot bear its complication),
today's *Buenos Aires Herald* reports Saddam's latest
ultimata, Bush's saber rattling, Shamir's self-righteous
told-you-so, and Arab ruptures
mere reason cannot patch.

       This hilltop
bench in the Plaza de San Martín affords no view of the gaudy
mausolea walled in Recoleta Cemetery
on the rise beyond. Yet surely, today as always, someone
has left a rose for Eva at the monument, where she
lies beside Papa Duarte and inspires
this neighborhood's spray-painting malcontent—
    Menem es traición
    Evita es resistencia—
to demand Peronism fulfill its contradictions.

As the fading light dissolves the view north into tinted
grains of old news photos, into silent frames of lost
maternal mansions still disintegrating
on great-grandfather's fragile nitrate,
the fine distinctions of mere reason pale.

End of the Line

A poem always lurks in the distance, hidden
   behind our best intentions, resisting
   notions of style, tradition, form—insisting
on having its own way, refusing to be bidden.

We recognize an end but don't know how
   to get there. We tell ourselves another lie
   rather than profess our failure to defy
the indefinable, the mystery, the now.

The "we" that speaks bespeaks community,
   as if to write, to sing, transcends this earth,
   transports the scribbler back to poetry's birth,
elevates to Parnassan heights aspiring clay.

But Orpheus could not outsing death's day,
   nor Apollo's lyre mortal grant immunity.

Pantoum: The Western Sky

Clouds loom over Chicago and the western sky.
Michigan's waters calm my nerves,
jangled by traffic and road construction.
I float belly-up and watch the circling gulls.

Michigan's waters calm my nerves.
The Lake swells gently, soothes me with its liquid sighs.
I float belly-up and watch the circling gulls.
They remind me of the voraciousness I've left behind.

The Lake swells gently, soothes me with its liquid sighs.
The sky's blue colors my thoughts a limpid azure.
They remind me of the voraciousness I've left behind—
Those gulls swooping and crying over head.

The sky's blue colors my thoughts a limpid azure.
I shut my eyes, rock to the waves, shut out the world.
Those gulls swooping and crying over head—
how can we satisfy such hunger?

I shut my eyes, rock to the waves, shut out the world
jangled by traffic and road construction.
How can we satisfy such hunger?
Clouds loom over Chicago and the western sky.

Rain

Rain pelts the screen of my office window
So hard I have to shut it for the first time
Since the start of classes: these bullet
Drops are straining to get in, but I won't
Have them swelling my file folders
Or diluting the handouts for my PM class.
Still, it's grand—the clicking, the ping
Of heaven coming to earth after such a dry spell.
Little wonder we have missed it, longed
To hear its beat, to awaken from the hum
Of the computer, the phone's beep, the electronic
Slumber into which we have been cast.
These leaden skies are promising, renew
Our arid lives: Before the sun, the dew.

Lifeguard

It is his habit, has always been,
to swim in the lane nearest the lifeguard,

to take his hour of laps in the slow lane
of the community pool, with its Olympic

proportions. His fellow swimmers
moving briskly a lane or two over

have, in the intimacy of the showers
and locker room, asked him why.

Though he is not so speedy as they,
they admire his stamina: He sustains

his Australian crawl, as old-timers say,
steadily through four laps, varied

by a fifth undertaken in an erratic
breast stroke and punctuated in the shallows

by a round of stretches to ward off
the cramps that plague his middle-aged limbs.

Two thousand meters he loops religiously,
steadily—so regular that the lifeguards

barely register his presence, following
instead the graceful butterflying

of mates on the swim team. But he
will not leave the senior crawlers,

whom he passes as traffic permits,

for a faster lane—one with the fit mother

who won the fifty-meter ribbon a quarter-
century ago or the septuagenarian who

rises to swim competitively during the dark
cold winters of the Northern Plains.

No, he remains close to those guards,
whose rotation marks the passage

of his hour, as his steady strokes mark off
the rhythmic striving of his life and days.

***

He prefers to avoid comparison—to ignore
the whippersnappers who usurp the slow lane,

as yet again they pass him hugging the wall
beneath the lifeguard's stand to let them by.

He wonders whether the guard can even see
how unfair youth is to age, floating and gloating

past their elders, who struggle to keep up, to persist.
Once upon a time his age would have suggested

the stage of life when years presaged sagacity.
But now no such presumption—it simply isn't so.

He hums a mnemonic melody keyed to the number
of his lap, "Heaven, I'm in heaven," for the rhyme

with eleven or "Uptown Girl" because he once argued
that downtown Manhattan started at 14th Street.

Some songs evoke an epoch or a love: "Time
after Time," the many years of marriage.

"Down to You," his undergraduate affair
with Joni Mitchell. "Old Times," the Diane

Keaton that Woody Allen taught him how to love.
"Love for Sale," not just because Ella and Anita

made it unforgettable but because the word it never
mentions (sex) helps him remember he's on lap

number six. That thought strikes home, strikes him
as middle-aged or worse. Yet each such strike's

a stroke—a stroke of luck, for every stroke
means that he is still here, still moving

forward to the wall, arm by arm, kick by kick,
forward in the hope that yet again he will return.

***

Longevity's his game, duration's
what he's after. So stroke follows

stroke: he pushes past fatigue,
raises his arm again and again and again,

glides for the umpteenth time through the shadow
cast by the lifeguard's stand. He notes whether

the guard is the same one he'd passed the last lap
and whether his protector is male or female—

an incidental detail that nonetheless intrigues him.
But he does not remark their age or color,

their hairstyle or attire. Why should he?
These attributes are, to him, irrelevant.

The swimmer needs the lifeguard for her skill,
for his know-how, for what he or she can do

to save the swimmer's life, to ensure he'll make it
up and down the lane—one arm raised over his head

as it swivels to the right for another inhalation,
which he then exhales into the chlorinated deep.

His is not the mystic circle of ideal nature, but
a stubborn linearity, an animal insistence. Again he

kicks, one more time he struggles to the wall, where
he turns, pushes off, heads back the way he came.

Back Porch: Northfield, MN

Squirrels and the red
note of cardinals

softened by screens—
Pollen silt—

A square of morning light—
On the white plastic table

a coffee cup, half full
an open book, face down

an uncapped pen—And the
empty Adirondack chair

Craft

Next to the study window, Dave Lemson
balances on a ladder and scrapes paint.
Chips are pinging off the screen far faster than
inspiration taps out words a poet can't
erase. Despite summer's swelter, Dave's up
to his eyeballs in flannel against sun
and mosquitoes. From booted toe to cap-top,
he inhabits his craft, wears his dedication.

Here at the computer I can't find rhyme
or reason for continuing this verse
in the face of such thorough application
to get things right. I just sigh every time
Dave descends and rises, stays his course—
a poet in bemused preoccupation.

Walk, Don't Run

Don't run on the pool deck
or in the slush-slick winter lobbies
of Minneapolis towers. Don't
run in the supermarket, where
you might smash your eggs—
or your neighbor's. Walk,
don't run, at the airport where
undue speed bespeaks terror.
Take your time: Slow down
for children and old folks, the hearing-
impaired and the blind, not to mention
the deer and the squirrels, the rabbits,
raccoons, and those strange swallow-like
birds that swoop unexpectedly out
of the fields and across the road right
in front of your car. Don't run
through the Abstract Expressionist
galleries at the Walker. Walk—
or you might miss a Kline
or a Motherwell. Walk, don't run
to your grandmother's coffin, to your intended
at the end of the aisle, and even into your
lover's arms. Walk, don't run—or someone
might get hurt. Walk, don't run—or you
might not remember how you got here.

Mnemosyne

For my mother

Without Memory the Muses pale, sink
from Parnassus into Oblivion,
Improvisation loses its jazzy sync-
opation, and Art the forms that fashion
Truth and Beauty from pigment and mere clay.
The Great Mother daily works her wonders,
transforms a supper into ritual stay
against confusion or the rattling hearse.

But her magic resides in *things* recalled:
a tuna casserole, a Friday lunch,
maternal hands seeking ease in Mozart
sonatas, while children (all ears now) crunch
the rice crisped against the Pyrex bowl—
simple monuments, mundane beaux-arts.

Villanelle: Mortality's an Everyday Affair

Mortality's an everyday affair—
Revealed in old folks' wrinkles and false teeth.
Death won't desert us, whatever we may dare.

Shopping won't help, nor altruistic care
Lavished on some unsuspecting grief:
Mortality's an everyday affair.

We doubt our meaning, though each word speaks fair,
Gives light and heart and promises relief:
Death won't desert us, whatever we may dare.

We groom ourselves, pomade our graying hair,
Conquer decay by jogging through the heath—
Mortality's an everyday affair.

We gaze into the mirror—and see what there?
The faulty image of our own belief?
Death won't desert us, whatever we may dare.

It's not a burden we may with others share,
Nor some spirit that waits upon our breath.
No, mortality's an everyday affair:
Death won't desert us, whatever we may dare.

Return to Me

silence
the maples are turning
burnt orange
whispers along the walk

silence
the gold is falling
red ash
crimsons the path

silence
the whole world is leaving
bronzed gilded
incarnadine

silence
leaf dust
return to me

Familial Rites: The Wedding

After years in exile, I'm drawn again into this circle,
for time quells even the terrors of Long Island.

My literally little, my only sister,
Today's bride,
commander now of priests who stipulate
Catholic ceremonies she reviews, revises, re-invents—
Cathy crosses toward me
after the whirl with uncle, father, brothers;
she crosses toward me,
her face blushing, mine in return, our common blood;
parting the crowd,
spinning America to ancient Cana's rhythm,
Catherine comes to me,
in nineteenth-century ivory,
her features recalling those unconverted before us—
the regal presence of our childhood matriarch,
our "Dearma," Ethel, our mother's mother's mother.

She is dancing to me
as the ghetto women never danced,
until they braved new worlds;
she is dancing with me
to eastern music, old Balkan sounds
a Catholic band plays now to please
our families both faithful and converted.

On our eclectic island home
we are dancing as our ancestors would have,
had the women been allowed, the times less trying;
we are dancing to the barking leader;
we are dancing to the applause of neighbors, friends, kin,
to sentiment, laughter, our own brief history,
to things remembered and forsaken—
warm milk tested on a childish wrist for an infant mouth:

We dance an irretrievable past, momently captive to our steps,
we dance and she
sweeps me
sweeps me back
sweeps me back into our circle.

In Search of Poetry

I keep searching memory—
an old map, the key to a route forward—
trying to remember the way to Dickinson's
room and the library at Whitman and Eliot.

I keep seeking the spot where Williams, Will,
and Bishop intersect—a backwater,
the no-place of a literary ghost town,
boarded up, far from the commercial highway.

I keep waiting for Ginsberg
to show up, fat with visionary lines
creasing his American face, glasses askew—
the very image of the place I want to be.

But today I go out. I hold an empty notebook.
Beneath a stark blue winter sky, the decorative
beech the city planted on the easement extends
its bare black branches—lines of poetry on air.

A Visit to Theresienstadt

1

When the prison became overcrowded
they added this room, smaller than the first floor
of my house—bare wooden pallets stacked
three high against the longer sides, shelves
for six hundred human ghosts. So many
died right here in fate's anteroom, even before
reaching death's chamber at the end of the line.

Now the room is stark—grayish-white floor and walls,
suffused light, the brown of dried wood. Dust
has settled over everything—no sign of loosened
bowels or the condensation of diseased breath
sliming the walls and floor. And no ghosts—no
great uncles, no distant cousins. Just
the relief of having escaped this fate
before it was even imaginable.

2

All those dead bodies—
there's no getting around
them, over them.
No step, no stride, so large.
My friends and I understand

the past but do not know where
to put these dead, these bodies,
how to pay them homage, how
to atone for so many lost, as if
right living could undo death.

3

We surrender to the shadow,
for now silence must suffice—
the murmur of the downpour
against the bus's windowpanes.
Bohemian hills, rich green, gold
rapeseed, mottled by clouds
and light, soften the split, the ragged
edge of conscience.

The bus moves along the new
highway toward Prague. *This too
shall pass.* We glide toward
the Old City. It's all new
to us, all as ephemeral
as the memory of the dead.

Autobiography: After Frank O'Hara

When I was a child,
I played under the Steinway
with my brothers and sister.
It was our cottage.

We lived there, orphaned
but self-sufficient. We hid
sandwiches and apples
in its crannied underbelly.

I did not tell my mother
or father how we thrived
in this world without them.
Nor about the food.

And here I am, on
the verge—for real
this time—of
orphanhood.

plenty

each morning
we toast
the bread
of unhappiness
butter it thick
with remorse

at noon
we linger
over a bowl
of procrastination
and relish
backsliding

each evening
we salt
regrets
and down
despair

we are lucky
we live in a land of plenty

New York School Cool

I'd like to write a poem like Frank O'Hara, but
I don't know Billie Holiday and don't hang out
in the Village. Hanging out at the Blue Monday
down on Division's not the same as grooving
to Charlie Parker at Birdland. Nor is listening
to a band at The Contented Cow from the promenade
by the Cannon like catching up with friends
at a Soho Gallery. Lunching with Becky in Northfield
is nice but not the same as running into Jasper Johns
or Willem de Kooning at a Village hot spot. Twenty-first
century Northfield just isn't Manhattan in the Fifties—
or even Brooklyn now. It needs another kind of poetry:
The music of pick-ups honking on a Friday night.
The chiaroscuro of college kids smoking on the sidewalk
by Ragstock. The flow of high school skateboarders
in Raiders ski caps as they circle elders, who hobble
purposefully behind their walkers. The mesmerizing
surge of the falls by the old Ames Mill. The buzzing
bees at noon in Bridge Square and cardinals flashing
red in the lilacs by the porch.

Geezers at the Old Saloon

For Bill

Two nascent fogies decided to forgo
sleeping at their desks one afternoon:
like Hemingway in Key West or out on the high seas
with el jefe Fidel in the good ol' days,
they would knock off a couple of rounds
before going home to their castles.

Or maybe not. Hemingway may have lived
longer than they, but not by much—and he came
to a grisly end. Fidel has lasted longer but is looking
the worse for wear. These two are seeking thrills
closer to home, discussing their gout and sipping
1919 root beer and a diet Coke. Papa H. would roll

over in his grave: so this is what has become
of a man's world? Worse, they're discussing
their wives' ups and downs as if the women
really mattered. They don't seem to miss
the beer or the tequila or the worm. The ex-wrestler
wonders whether he should sauté chicken livers

in the Cajun mode for his wife's supper,
while the chubby nervous one worries that his spouse's
angst may give her (or is it him?) *angina pectoris*.
Yet they seem happy, sipping their good
fortune: their friendship, the women whom they
love, this afternoon adventure at the old saloon.

O Mortal Raisin!

My morning raisins had a lustrous,
Royal-purple past. But withered now,
Shriveled and dead, they have become
Another's cold repast—not food
For worms, but mere feed for us poor
Cattle on whom the worms will, when
We've ripened, soon or later feast.
That is the raisin's *raison d'être*—
To recall to us our common
Proper end: We blithe, vivacious
Creatures too readily forget all
Die that others—high and low—may
Fly or swim or, like us, crawl
The earth, brief festival of living clay.

The Lost Book of Hours

We worked by the old seasonal clock reversed:
fall for planting, winter for growth,
spring for harvesting—summer, our day of rest.
But now Boards of Higher Learning demand accountability,
so budget and grade sheet, bottom line and cutback,
replace the rhythms of academic cultivation.
There is no going back to medieval gowns,
candlelight contemplation, uninterrupted illumination.

Even here we've replaced the bells with buzzers,
computed ourselves into every equation,
installed escalators to the top of ivory towers.

Productivity orchestrates our labors, thoughts
lost in the hustle and bustle of exchanged ideas—
our mental currency, the bits and bytes of commerce.

The Would-be Naturalist Goes Birding

So those four eagles I saw yesterday—
they turned out to be turkey vultures,
circling low over the pond and the field,
tilting and shimmying on a brisk wind.

It felt a little like the loss of patriotism
back when I was in college and Nixon
fired Archibald Cox and proved he was
the presidential liar I'd denied he was.

Mistaking those vultures for eagles—losing
those damned eagles—felt like losing faith
in the one holy, catholic, and apostolic
church. All over again. Wasn't once enough?

So this morning I went out with an urbane
biologist who admitted he wasn't sure either
about the bird that swooped down over us,
scavenging, its eye peeled for something

to fill its maw, like Nixon, not trusting
the democracy he believed he was defending
to give him the votes he needed, and so grabbing
them instead. Nature's hunger, American greed—

you understand better, after eagles disappear,
turn vulture, that we live among the dead,
that large black wings cast shadows over us—
harbingers of grief, those night-dark silhouettes.

Northern Winter

Here in the northland, night's shadow lengthens
into light. On warm winter days snow-clad
eaves metamorphose drop by drop into the clear
cold fangs of darkness. Night is always near.

The solstitial chill feeds on snow's reflected
light. Cardinals, redder than remembrance,
fly—silent simulacra of the living,
vermilion life surviving on the wing.

On coldest days searing blue light abounds,
arises everywhere, blinds every creature—
as cruel to sight as to the eye the razor's edge.
Icicles and snow pack crack, acknowledge

winter's dominion. Dull cold shadow of life,
earth holds its breath still, still, for spring's green strife.

Charlie Chaplin Jumps the Median

In the movie, of course, Charlie
Chaplin would jump the median,
the Model A rolling over several
times and landing wheels up
and spinning. The Little Tramp
would crawl out the passenger's
side window, dust himself off,
fetch his bowler from the wreck,
and waddle down the sloping
road and across the bridge—a long,
slow shot that holds him and us
until he disappears.

But that's not, of course, what
happens. In reality, the wreck's
a wreck; the Tramp, a late middle-
aged guy trying to make ends
meet in very bad times. Some very
young National Guardsmen—
en route to weekend maneuvers
at the nearby base—see the car
spin on invisible black ice, tip
over as it crests the median,
and come to rest against the barrier
at the top of the hill by the underpass.
It could, they think, have been worse.

They help him out, call 9-1-1, wait
with him. He feels older than
his half century but grateful
for their solicitude. The boys
leave (for Afghanistan, in the end?)
when the cops come, who in turn
surrender to a state trooper,

a tow-truck, and a winch.

The Tramp isn't hurt but doesn't
duck-walk across the bridge.
The trooper drops him, with a box
of stuff from the car, accumulated
over years, at the light rail. He rides
to work as if on a normal day, meets
his class on time, laughs with students
about his brush with fate and about
their classmate, who's been bemoaning
how destiny denied her a timely parking
spot and how awful her morning's been.

For the moment he's alive. He's fully
present to them and to himself. He feels
the here-ness of being here. For a moment
he forgets the hidden hand that drove
him over the median, losses that make
him wish the end had not been happy:

His father—shaking with Parkinson's.
His mother, fretting, feeding her husband
pill after pill, denying the inevitable end.
The sister—broke again and trapped
in a loveless marriage. His favorite niece,
drunk nightly. His son, darkening within.
His sad, sad wife, sighing into oblivion.

The Little Tramp's resilience—it's a trick
of the cinematic eye, a play of light
and shadow on a blank screen. It's the triumph
of illusion over reality and it isn't enough—or fair:
Charlie Chaplin walks out of the wreckage.

Parting Glances

After Bill Sherwood

So late to the airport
there's no time for crying.
I watch her cross the tar-mac
turn to wave
once halfway to the aircraft,
once, at the top of the stairs, just before entering—
a graceful Jackie Kennedy turn—
then red hair
framed by the exit window over the wing.
Props start and stop,
stop and start:
she taxis away.

Two weeks later I'm so lonely
my other half rises.
So of course I go to a film instead.
In downtown Dayton, at the art house,
two men on screen are kissing:
they mean more than sex.
Later the KKK (incognito) and the bikers
gape at the audience departing—
men kissing men on the street,
women arm in arm.

Love's so tempting
I run off
green and glowing
through Ohio thunder and lightning and air
thick with the last rain
expecting the next—
off to the mall
where boys heckle me for shouldering a bag

no one would notice back East.

When I pass a mirror I look
to see myself
as she does

framed by the terminal window
and deserving love.

Gratitude

1: *Le Chaim*

Each day, my own sunrise, my own morning star:
your red head radiates strange aerial spikes.

Our son's beard and long Hasidic locks
on a head never bowed in prayer hover

over his guitar and, till he gets it just so,
a heavy-metal riff. The picture of Ollie, our old pup,—

his face speaks love, love, love. Like the holiday meal
you'll pretend to let me cook. Or when your hand gently

strokes my heaving shoulder: I am sobbing silently
because the movie has ended well—a good death,
timely reconciliation, vows revived, a renewed breath.

2. In Praise of Delusion

When he walks down the sloping skyway from Memorial
to the Music building on his way to a long evening class,
he sees his reflection in the large classroom window
at the base of the slope. He loves that mirror.
In it, he is about a foot taller than his five-five-and-a-half
and twenty pounds lighter. He is younger than his sixty years.
The silver hair is less telling. As he approaches, the other
sways slightly, moves with the elegant gait of an athlete
or dancer. *This*, he imagines, *is my Norwegian double—
tall and slender and (at least from this distance) good-looking.*
Of course as man and image converge, his other shrinks
into an eastern-European, Semitic, rather compact, little old man.
Perhaps (he wonders) *I have seen the inner image of myself.*
Perhaps (he smiles) *I am happy just to have illusions.*

3. Thanksgiving

This morning, as I drive
from Northfield to Hampton
past field after barren field,
three wild turkeys

foraging and gobbling
at the edge of the road—
their white-splashed wings,
black-feathered trunks,

red combs poking
and pecking the gravel
and weeds—surprise me.

I flinch.
        The car swerves.
I breathe.
        They range unruffled.

4: To My Son

It's Friday, Z—, and (as always) time to say how much I love you (and your mom too, since I don't say it often enough though I feel it every minute) and how much I miss you and hope you can spend a few hours with us and Grandma the first weekend in November. We worry about you every day, 'cuz that's our job, but we also have an abiding sense of how strong you are: How much you have been through, how far you've come, and how you face each day with grit—and, I hope, love. The latter is so hard to do: Over breakfast your mom and I sometimes sit around and whine about our work, about grading student papers. But a little later I'll be walking across campus and the light will be just right and I'll see a familiar face amid a group of young people and—I don't know why—I feel love. I think that's the word. And I felt it last time we picked you up downtown and you were talking to some scruffy stranger on the street. And the fact that you can still be open to such encounters—isn't that love too?—filled me with wonder. It's funny: Old people, among whom I am about to number, have proverbially been beyond wonder, such a romantic and old-fashioned word. But I swear that I still feel it—and that you are among the wonders of my world.

A Topography of Love

For Becky

Just as erosion and receding glaciers
have sculpted alpine grandeur and the majesty
of canyons, so Time has scarred our flesh.
It has chronicled our obsession
with the Question—to eat or not to eat?—
and etched tracks of crowing laughter
and ravens of despair about our eyes.

Your breast and belly the surgeon's knife
haunts still, as do the stretch and sag of pregnancy.
Your body lives the history of our love
more richly and more beautifully than this lover
or any could deserve. Our passion feeds
on liver spots, *los besos de amor*.

You are becoming the woman I have
always loved and perversely ever longed for.
Your once fiery hair, though dimmed by age's ash,
still consumes my sight, still dazzles me.
I love you with a love I cannot utter
in words I cannot write
beyond the thousand shocks that flesh is heir to.

"You are the world to me,"
we say when we are young.
But worlds are not created in a day.
They emerge slowly out of chaos,
like ancient lovers turning in their sleep.

ABOUT THE AUTHOR

D. E. (Doug) Green teaches literature, creative writing, composition, and gender and queer studies at Augsburg University. He has published many articles on Shakespeare, regular reviews of productions for *Shakespeare Bulletin*, general-interest essays, and poetry. His poem "Gratitude" won the 2017 Martin Lake Journal Bookend Prize. His poems also appear on the sidewalks of Northfield, MN, where he lives with his spouse, writer Becky Boling. Doug likes to say that he has been an occasional poet for over 35 years.

www.ingramcontent.com/pod-product-compliance
Lightning Source LLC
Chambersburg PA
CBHW060411080526
44583CB00012B/529